SCHOLA

Learning Express

Handwriting and Vocabulary

This book belongs to

Welcome to Learning Express!

Helping your child build essential skills is easy!

These teacher-approved activities have been specially developed to make learning both accessible and enjoyable. On each page, you'll find:

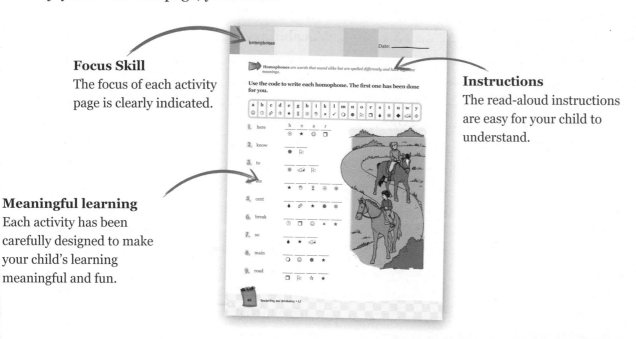

Focus Skill
The focus of each activity page is clearly indicated.

Instructions
The read-aloud instructions are easy for your child to understand.

Meaningful learning
Each activity has been carefully designed to make your child's learning meaningful and fun.

This book also contains:

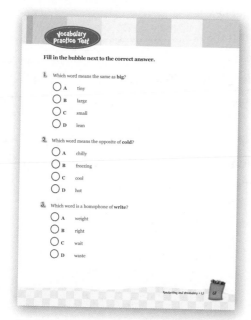

Instant assessment to ensure your child really masters the skills.

Completion certificate to celebrate your child's leap in learning.

Motivational stickers to mark the milestones of your child's learning path.

Contents

Alphabet and Handwriting

"Look, I'm writing words!" Once your child begins to put letters together to form words, the magic of making words and sentences begins.

In this section, your child will use upper- and lowercase letters of the alphabet to write sentences. He or she will also learn frequently used words, including the days of the week, the months of the year and animal names.

What to do
Encourage your child to trace and then write the letters and sentences on each page. Review his or her work. Compliment your child on carefully formed letters.

Keep On Going!
Have your child practice writing by having him or her write notes to family and friends. The notes might tell about a favorite movie or exciting plans coming up, such as a visit to the zoo.

Date: _____

A a

Trace and write.

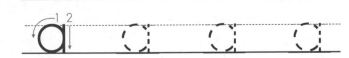

Aa

Adam Ape is active.

Annie asked Alice.

B b

Trace and write.

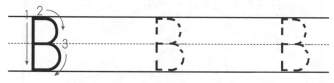

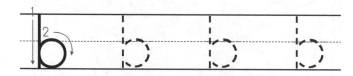

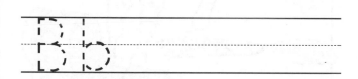

Betsy bee buzzes.

Bobby buys balloons.

Date: _____

Cc

Trace and write.

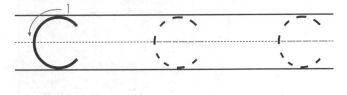

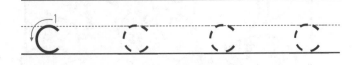

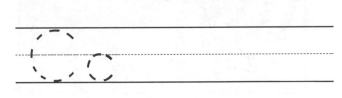

Cows crave color.

Callie carries cats.

Date: _____

D d

Trace and write.

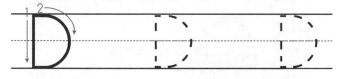

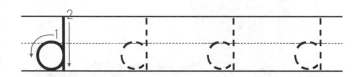

D d

Dandy Duck dances.

Dragons draw dogs.

Date: _____

E e

Trace and write.

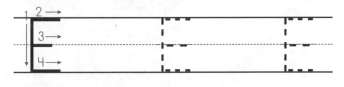

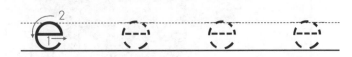

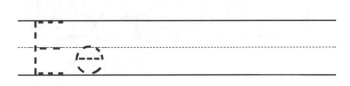

Ellie Emu is elegant.

Ed eats eight eggs.

Date: _____

F f

Trace and write.

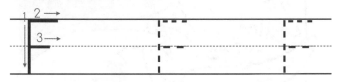

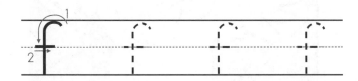

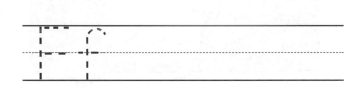

Fran Fish is funny.

Footballs fly fast.

Date: _____

Gg

Trace and write.

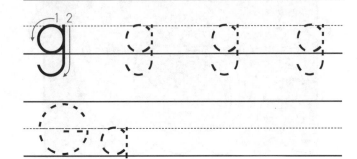

Hee
Hee Hee

Gus Goose giggles.

Greta grows greens.

Date: _____

Hh

Trace and write.

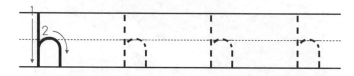

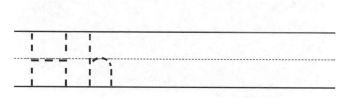

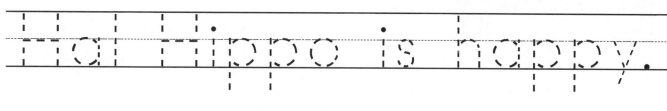

Hal Hippo is happy.

Hannah hangs hats.

Date: _____

Ii

Trace and write.

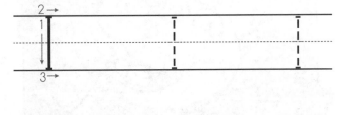

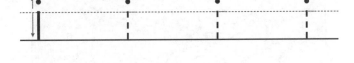

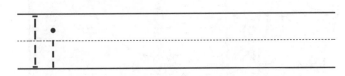

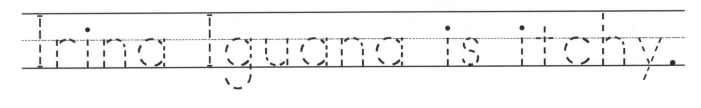

Irina Iguana is itchy.

Invite Irving inside.

Date: _____

Jj

Trace and write.

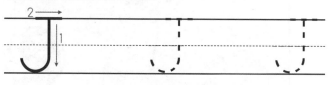

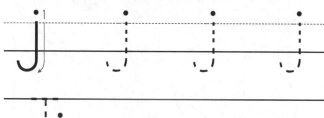

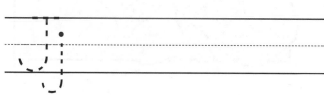

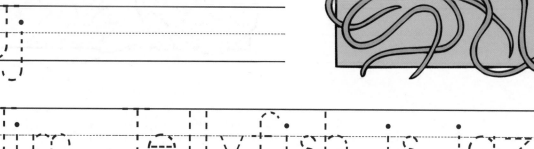

Jim Jellyfish is jazzy.

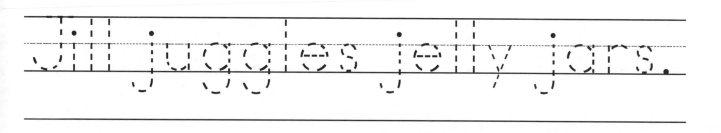

Jill juggles jelly jars.

Date: _____

K k

Trace and write.

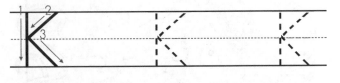

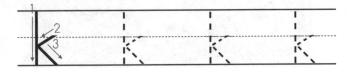

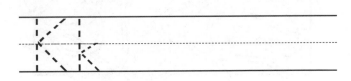

Kyle Kangaroo kicks.

Katie keeps kittens.

Date: _____

L l

Trace and write.

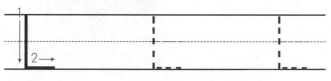

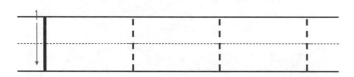

Lyle Lion looks lost.

Lindy loves lollipops.

Date: _____

Mm

Trace and write.

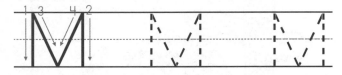

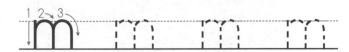

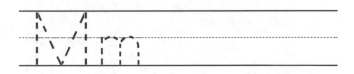

Mm

Mike Mouse is messy.

Mom meets Mag.

Date: _____

Nn

Trace and write.

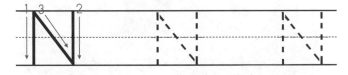

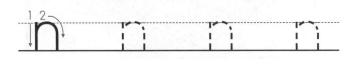

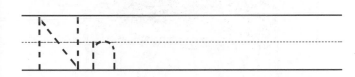

Nikki Newt needs naps.

Nurse Ned nibbles.

Date: _____

Trace and write.

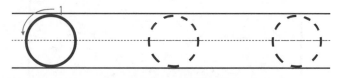

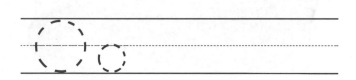

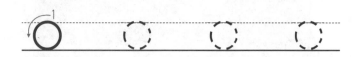

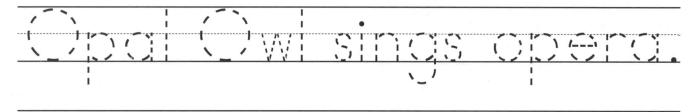

Opal Owl sings opera.

Otis orders oranges.

Date: _____

Pp

Trace and write.

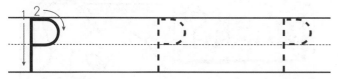

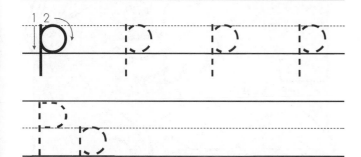

Pip Penguin is playful.

Peter Parrot says please.

Date: _____

Q q

Trace and write.

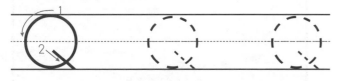

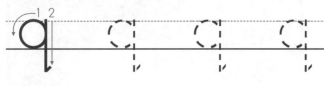

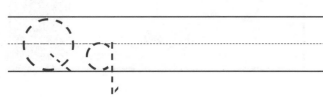

Quinn Quail is quiet.

Quincy has a quilt.

Date: _____

Rr

Trace and write.

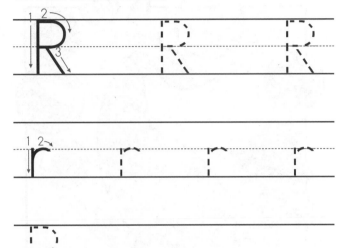

Ricky Rabbit races.

Robin reads rapidly.

Date: _____

S s

Trace and write.

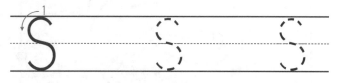

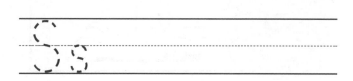

Susanna Seal stars.

Sam sees sailboats.

T t

Trace and write.

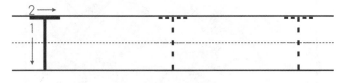

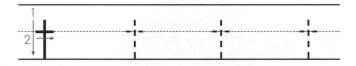

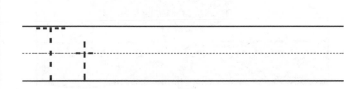

Tristan Toad is toothy.

Tigers taste terrible.

Date: _____

U u

Trace and write.

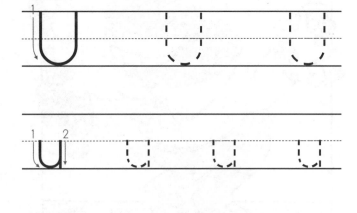

Uu uses an umbrella.

Uncle Uno umpires.

Date: _____

V v

Trace and write.

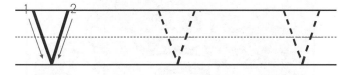

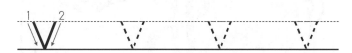

Vic Vulture is vain.

Vegetables vary.

Date: _____

Ww

Trace and write.

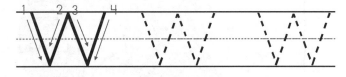

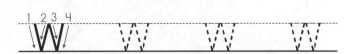

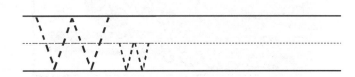

Will Worm is wealthy.

Wilma wipes windows.

Date: _____

X x

Trace and write.

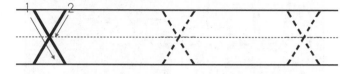

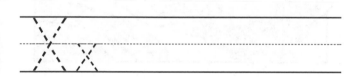

Xavier Fox is excited.

Xenia Ox exits.

Date: _____

Y y

Trace and write.

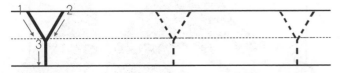

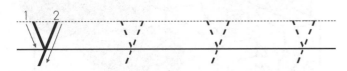

Yasmin Yak yawns.

Young yaks yodel.

Date: _____

Z z

Trace and write.

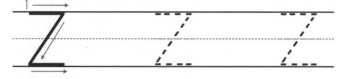

Zoe Zebra is zany.

Zed zooms at the zoo.

Date: _____

Trace and write the days of the week.

Sunday

Monday

Tuesday

Wednesday

Thursday

Friday

Saturday

Date: _____

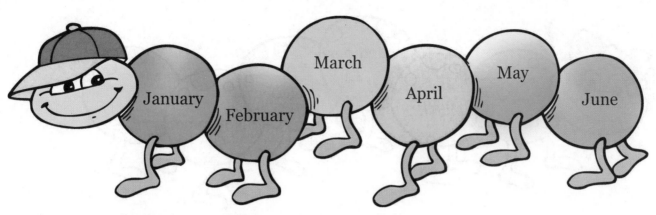

Trace and write the months of the year.

January

February

March

April

May

June

Date: _____

Trace and write the months of the year.

July

August

September

October

November

December

Date: _____

Write the names of the animals on the lines below.

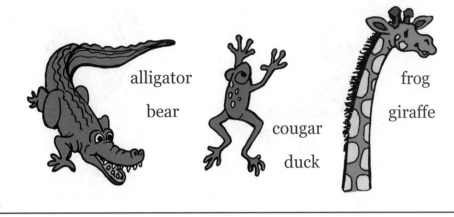

alligator

bear

cougar

duck

frog

giraffe

Date: _____

Write the names of the animals on the lines below.

iguana   leopard

jaguar   moose

kangaroo ostrich

_____

_____

_____

_____

_____

_____

_____

_____

_____

_____

Date: _____

Write the names of the animals on the lines below.

parrot

quail

raccoon

squirrel

tiger

urchin

Date: _____

Write the names of the animals on the lines below.

shark

vulture

whale

X-ray fish

yak

zebra

Alphabet Practice Test

Fill in the bubble next to the correct answer.

Example

Say the word. Which letter is the first letter of the word?

○ D

○ C

● A

○ F

---

 1. Say the word. Which letter is the first letter of the word?

○ T

○ E

○ R

○ D

---

 2. Say the word. Which letter is the last letter of the word?

○ E

○ P

○ N

○ T

Fill in the bubble next to the correct answer.

3.

e   f   ◻   h   i

Which letter is missing?

○ d

○ g

○ j

○ m

4.

◻   n   o   p   ◻   r   s

Which two letters are missing?

○ m and q

○ t and g

○ m and t

○ q and u

Vocabulary

Your child is introduced to a variety of words in this section. Building a strong vocabulary is an important step in becoming a fluent reader.

What to do

Have your child work on the activity pages. Review his or her work. Ask your child if he or she has learned new words. Encourage your child to add them to the Master Word List. Review the words on the list periodically.

Paste the flash cards on pages 71–76 onto cardboard or poster board. Then cut them out. Use them to build and reinforce vocabulary development.

Keep On Going!

Play a word game with your child. Say a word and ask your child to tell you an antonym (opposite) and a synonym (same meaning) for the word.

Synonyms *are words with the same or nearly the same meanings.*

Read each word at the top of the box. Circle every other letter. Write the letters in order on the line to spell a synonym. The first one is done for you.

1. begin

_____ start _____

2. glad

_____

3. loud

_____

4. little

_____

5. see

_____

6. big

_____

Date: _____

Circle every other letter. Write the circled letters in order on the line to name the synonym for each word. The first one has been done for you.

1. begin   s (s) y (t) n (a) o (r) n (t)   _____start_____

2. soft   y q m u s i a e r t   _____

3. tell   e s w a o y   _____

4. tale   r s d t s o t r h y   _____

5. correct   a r t i h g a h v t   _____

6. look   e p t e h e e k   _____

7. huge   s b a i m g   _____

8. fearful   e a m f e r a a n i i d   _____

9. group   n s g e s t   _____

Write the letters you did not circle in order on the blanks to complete the sentence.

_ _ _ _ _ _ _ _ _   _ _ _   _ _ _ _ _   _ _ _ _

_ _ _ _   _ _ _   _ _ _ _   _ _ _ _ _ _ _ _ .

Date: _____

Antonyms *are words with opposite meanings.*

Read the word on each flowerpot. Color the flower with the antonym.

1. **down** — up, under, over
2. **little** — bed, big, hot
3. **out** — in, on, down
4. **dry** — cut, boy, wet
5. **cold** — cool, water, hot
6. **under** — over, out, on
7. **hard** — soft, rough, neat
8. **clean** — silly, sad, dirty
9. **happy** — tall, sad, big

Date: _____

Write an antonym for each clue to complete the crossword puzzle. Use the words in the Word Box below to help you.

Across	Down
1. smile	2. new
4. right	3. south
6. clean	4. big
9. sad	5. last
11. start	7. close
12. wide	8. lost
14. rough	10. down
16. under	13. forget
	15. short

Word Box

tall	open
left	frown
first	found
old	smooth
stop	across
little	happy
over	remember
dirty	narrow
north	

Date: _____

 Compound words *are two words joined together to make a new word.*

Draw a line to join the boxes to make compound words. Write the compound word. The first one has been done for you.

door	hive
foot	flower
sun	time
cup	bell
bee	brush
bed	ball
flower	shelf
rain	cake
pop	corn
tooth	pot
book	coat

1. _____doorbell_____
2. _____
3. _____
4. _____
5. _____
6. _____
7. _____
8. _____
9. _____
10. _____
11. _____

Date: _____

 *A **compound word** is a word made by joining two words together to make a new word.*

Complete the crossword puzzle with the missing part of each compound word. Use the words in the Word Box to help you.

Word Box

lid	knob
bath	brush
hive	plane
down	flower
bed	shelf
finger	ground

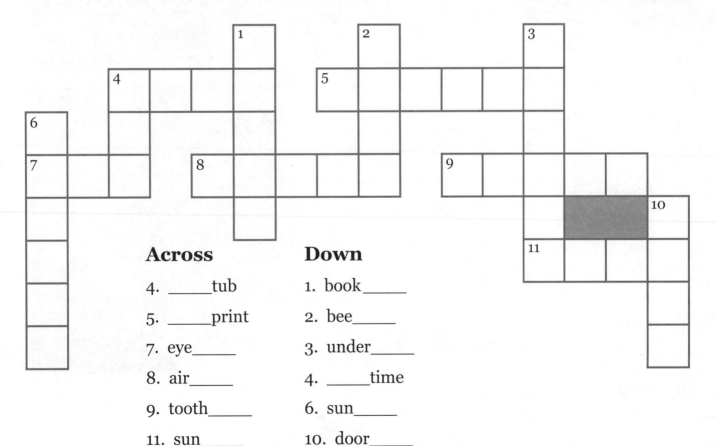

Across

4. _____tub
5. _____print
7. eye_____
8. air_____
9. tooth_____
11. sun_____

Down

1. book_____
2. bee_____
3. under_____
4. _____time
6. sun_____
10. door_____

Date: _____

 Homophones *are words that sound alike but are spelled differently and have different meanings.*

Use the code to write each homophone. The first one has been done for you.

a	b	c	d	e	g	h	i	k	l	m	n	o	r	s	t	u	w	y
☺	🕐	↪	☆	★	⧖	❀	✋	✗	✓	○	⊛	⚑	□	💧	❄	📬	◆	◈

1. here   <u>h</u> <u>e</u> <u>a</u> <u>r</u>
       ❀ ★ ☺ □

2. know   ___ ___
       ⊛ ⚑

3. to   ___ ___ ___
       ❄ 📬 ⚑

4. ate   ___ ___ ___ ___ ___
       ★ ✋ ⧖ ❀ ❄

5. cent   ___ ___ ___ ___ ___
       💧 ↪ ★ ⊛ ❄

6. break   ___ ___ ___ ___ ___
       🕐 □ ☺ ✗ ★

7. so   ___ ___ ___
       💧 ★ 📬

8. main   ___ ___ ___ ___
       ○ ☺ ⊛ ★

9. road   ___ ___ ___ ___
       □ ⚑ ☆ ★

Date: _____

Add or subtract letters to spell the homophone of the first word. Choose the homophone that fits each sentence and fill in the blanks. The first one has been done for you.

1. deer – er + ar = <u>dear</u>   The <u>deer</u> jumped the fence to safety.

2. two – w = _____   A duet is made of _____ singers.

3. sun – u + o = _____   The father took his _____ to the game.

4. scent – s = _____   The _____ of flowers filled the room.

5. chili – i + ly = _____   Wear a coat when it is _____.

6. their – ir + re = _____   We can go _____ on a holiday.

7. know – k – w = _____   The sign says _____ swimming.

8. hair – ir + re = _____   Brush your _____ before going to school.

9. bee – e = _____   The _____ buzzed around in the garden.

10. here – re + ar = _____   They could _____ the traffic outside.

Date: _____

Homonyms *are words that have more than one meaning.*

Write the word from a star that can be used in both blanks in each sentence. The first one has been done for you.

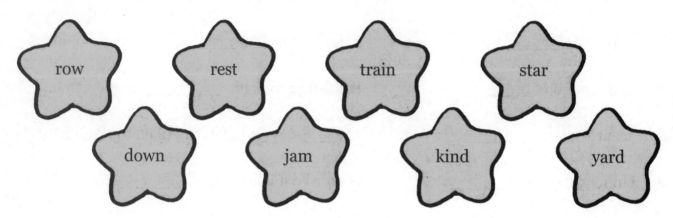

1. The ____star____ of the team won the medal with a gold ____star____.

2. The _____ of boats were all ready to _____ to the finish line.

3. We found a _____ of ribbon while playing in the _____.

4. Juan threw the _____ pillow _____ from the top bunk.

5. Amber wanted to _____ before finishing the _____ of her homework.

6. The _____ woman let me choose my favorite _____ of ice cream.

7. Christy needs to _____ her dog before they ride on the _____.

8. Scott ate toast and _____ during the traffic _____.

Date: _____

Unscramble the shape words. Use the words in the Word Box to help you. Write the words on the lines.

Word Box

diamond
square
octagon
triangle
rectangle
circle

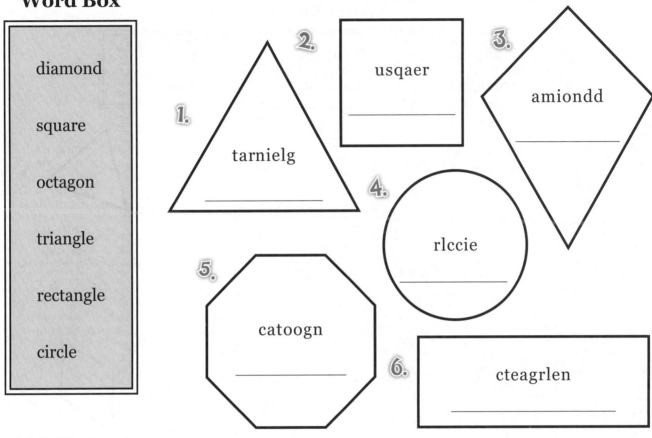

1. tarnielg _____

2. usqaer _____

3. amiondd _____

4. rlccie _____

5. catoogn _____

6. cteagrlen _____

What shape is a ...

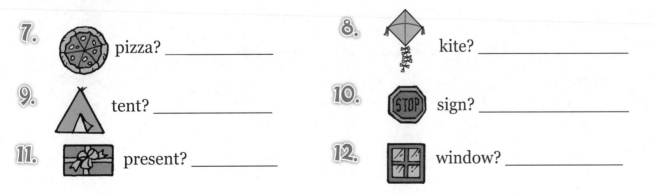

7. pizza? _____

8. kite? _____

9. tent? _____

10. sign? _____

11. present? _____

12. window? _____

 Find eight things in your home that are shaped like a rectangle. Name them.

Date: _____

Unscramble each shape word and write it on the line. Use the words in the Word Box to help you. Then match each shape word to the shape. Color each shape.

Word Box

circle	rectangle	oval
triangle	diamond	square

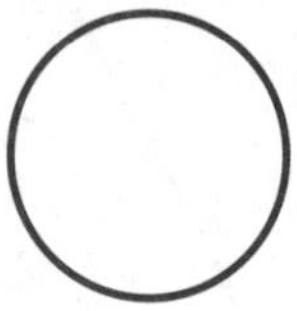

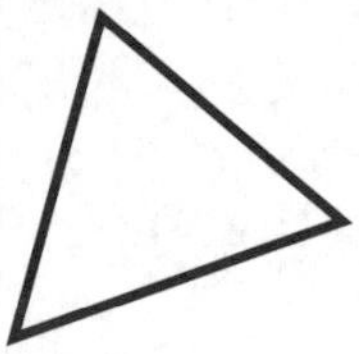

1. suqera _____
   red

2. tigaelrn _____
   white

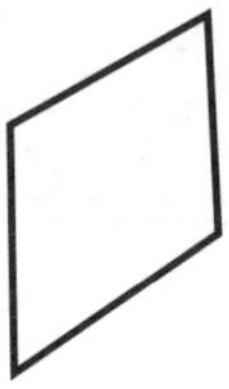

3. anreclget _____
   black

4. addmoin _____
   green

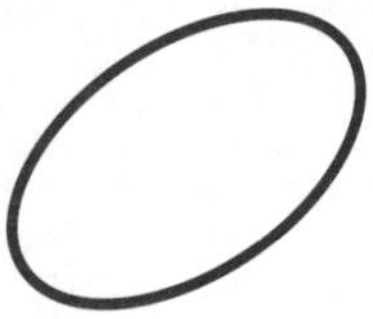

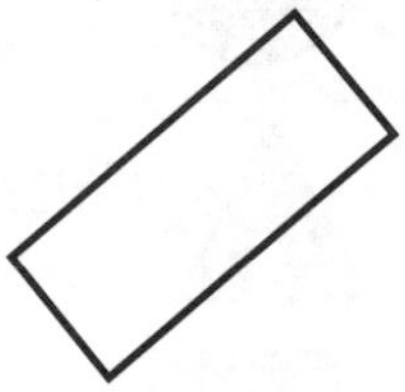

5. lvoa _____
   yellow

6. rcclie _____
   brown

Date: _____

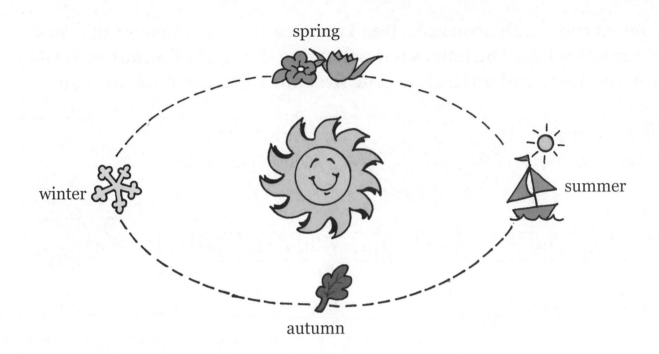

spring

winter

summer

autumn

Circle the season that goes with each sentence.

1. The weather becomes very hot.

2. Children build snowmen.

3. Leaves turn red, orange and yellow.

4. Children go swimming outside.

5. Flowers begin to bloom.

6. Trees start losing leaves.

Date: _____

Look at the weather picture. Read the weather clue. Cross out every other letter box. The letters left will name the kind of weather. Write the weather word on the line. The first one has been done for you.

I see nothing but snow.

b	e	l	n	i	s	z	a	z	i	a	d	r	t	d

1. _____blizzard_____

I see balls of ice falling from the sky.

h	j	a	j	i	q	l

2. _____

I see a dark funnel cloud in the sky.

t	r	o	p	r	b	n	g	a	j	d	u	o

3. _____

I see water drops falling from the sky.

r	g	a	k	i	a	n

4. _____

I see white flakes falling from the sky.

s	e	n	b	o	i	w

5. _____

I see beautiful blue skies.

s	f	u	s	n	c	s	l	h	o	i	r	n	r	e

6. _____

Date: _____

Read each clue. Write the names of the correct animals in the crossword puzzle.

alligator

dolphin

penguin

bear

ape

octopus

lion

Across

2. This mammal hibernates in the winter.

5. This reptile has a long nose and sharp teeth.

6. This mammal lives in the forest.

7. This mammal has a mane.

Down

1. This bird uses its wings to swim.

3. This mammal lives like a fish.

4. This sea creature has eight arms.

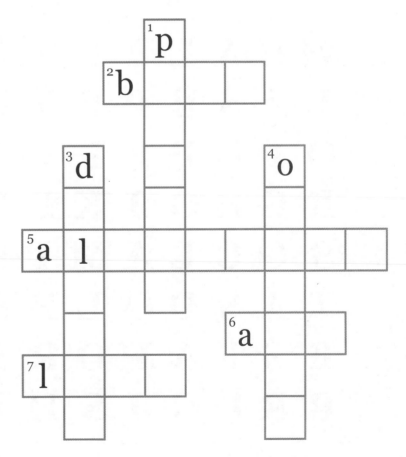

Date: _____

**Spot and circle the words from the Word Box in the puzzle below.
The words go across and down.**

Word Box

WHALE	SHARK
FISH	EEL
CLAM	SHRIMP
LOBSTER	TURTLE
DOLPHIN	SEAHORSE

```
W H A L E E T S Z C T F
L A S E P E Y H B X U I
O F D P R L V A N M R S
B G H O J K L R E K T H
S O C L A M I K U Y L T
T A S D O L P H I N E D
E S E A H O R S E G H F
R R D G J S H R I M P T
```

Date: _____

Spot and circle the words from the Word Box in the puzzle below. The words go across and down.

Word Box

bee	roach
mosquito	beetle
ant	ladybug
grasshopper	moth
cricket	butterfly

```
g r a s s h o p p e r c
b w e r l a d y b u g r
e y b u t t e r f l y i
e u i k m n a n t b f c
m o t h l j k u y s a k
r t e q a r o a c h o e
b e e t l e y s i m p t
n f h j m o s q u i t o
```

Date: _____

Cross out every other letter to name the baby animal. Write the name on the line. The first one has been done for you.

| k | j | i | u | t | g | t | b | e | s | n |

1. ___kitten___

| l | v | a | g | m | c | b |

2. _____

| t | h | a | t | d | a | p | k | o | r | l | f | e |

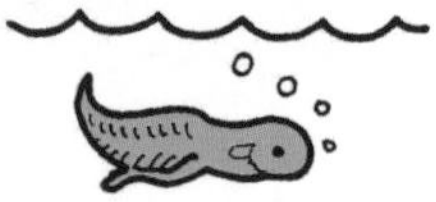

3. _____

| d | f | u | j | c | w | k | d | l | n | i | k | n | o | g |

4. _____

| f | c | a | i | w | d | n |

5. _____

| c | e | u | x | b |

6. _____

| c | l | a | d | l | n | f |

7. _____

| f | d | o | h | a | y | l |

8. _____

| c | o | h | r | i | e | c | q | k |

9. _____

| p | b | u | u | p | a | p | z | y |

10. _____

Date: _____

Read each clue. Write the name of each community helper.

1. I give you a checkup each year as you grow up.

___ ___ ___ ___ ___
          5

2. I drive a vehicle that is really cool. I pick you up each day for school.

___ ___ ___   ___ ___ ___ ___ ___ ___
     6

3. When smoke hits your nose I'll come with my hose.

___ ___ ___ ___ ___ ___ ___ ___ ___ ___ ___
               2

4. I work on your teeth awhile, so you can have a bright smile.

___ ___ ___ ___ ___ ___ ___
       4

5. I share a lot for you to learn, and in my class we all take turns.

___ ___ ___ ___ ___ ___ ___
  1

6. I am here to help you look for an interesting book.

___ ___ ___ ___ ___ ___ ___ ___ ___
              3

Use the letters from above to finish the sentence.

For all that you do, we say . . .

___ ___ ___ ___k y___ ___!
1   2   3   4   5 6

bus driver	doctor	dentist
librarian	firefighter	teacher

Date: _____

Circle the transportation words in the letter grid. The words go across and down.

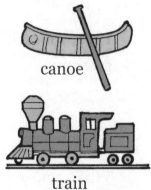
canoe

airplane

sailboat

van

s	h	i	p	a	n	a
a	e	t	d	o	b	i
i	l	s	v	a	i	r
l	i	t	a	k	k	p
b	c	a	n	o	e	l
o	o	e	r	c	f	a
a	p	u	c	a	r	n
t	t	r	u	c	k	e
r	e	v	h	b	u	s
t	r	a	i	n	l	s

train

car

truck

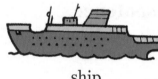
bus

ship

helicopter

bike

Complete the chart to identify different kinds of transportation.

air	land	water
_____	_____	_____
_____	_____	_____
	_____	_____
	_____	
	_____	

Date: _____

Use the code to fill in the blanks about parts of a map.

a	b	c	e	h	k	l	m	n	o	p	r	s	t	u	w	y
↙	❈	○	❄	●	✪	✧	☑	⇒	✿	⚙	⌒	◀	⊙	⏱	☺	↗

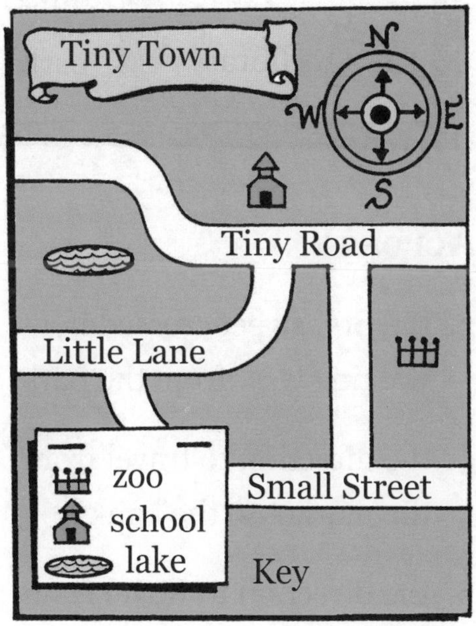

1. A map __ __ __ __ __ __ is a
   ◀ ↗ ☑ ❈ ✿ ✧

   picture that stands for a real thing.

2. A list of symbols and what they stand

   for is called the __ __ __ __ __ __.
   ☑ ↙ ⚙ ✪ ❄ ↗

3. The cardinal directions are

   __ __ __ __ __, __ __ __ __ __,
   ⇒ ❈ ⌒ ● ● ◀ ✿ ⏱ ⊙ ●

   __ __ __ __ and __ __ __ __.
   ❄ ↙ ◀ ⊙   ☺ ❄ ◀ ⊙

4. The __ __ __ __ __ __ __ __ __ __ __
   ○ ✿ ☑ ⚙ ↙ ◀ ◀   ● ✿ ◀ ❄

   shows the cardinal directions on a map.

Date: _____

Use the map and the Word Box to complete the crossword puzzle.

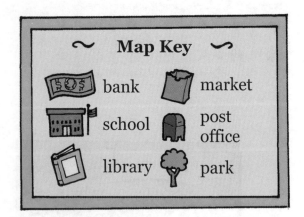

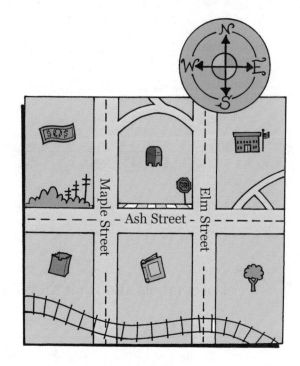

Across

3. the first street crossed if walking west from the park

5. the direction to travel from the market to the bank

6. the direction to travel from the post office to the school

Word Box

north	south	east	west

Down

1. the direction to travel from the library to the market

2. the first street crossed if walking east from the bank

4. the direction to travel from the school to the park

7. the street crossed if walking north from the library

Date: _____

Use a word from the Word Box to describe the character trait shown in each picture.

Word Box

| polite | cooperative | helpful | honest | hard-working | kind |

1. I have finished my homework.

   1. _____

2. Sir, I think you dropped some money.

   2. _____

3. Dad, I'll take out the trash.

   3. _____

4. We make a good team!

   4. _____

5. Would you like one of my cookies?

   5. _____

6. Thank you for the ice cream, Mom.

   6. _____

Date: _____

An **analogy** *is a comparison between two things that are similar in some respects.*

Finish each analogy using a word from the Word Box. Write the word on the line.

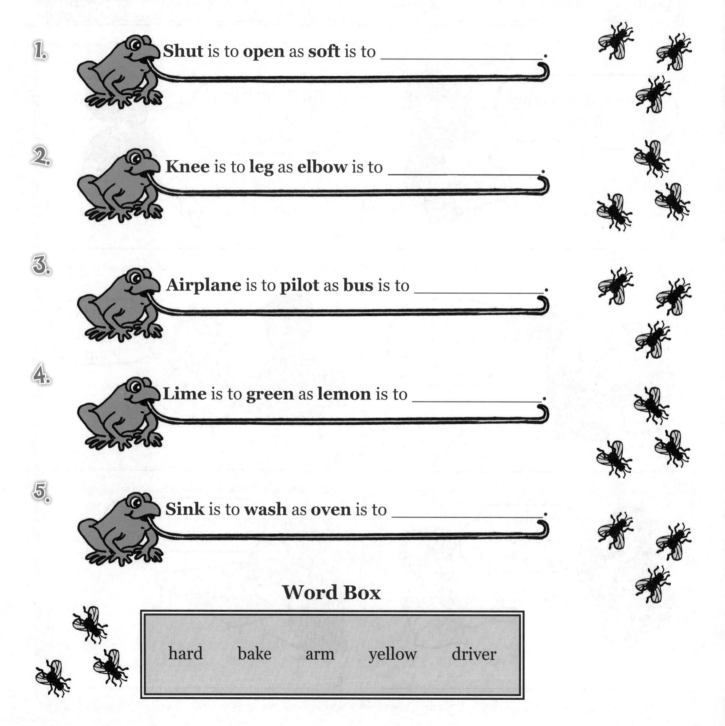

1. **Shut** is to **open** as **soft** is to _____.

2. **Knee** is to **leg** as **elbow** is to _____.

3. **Airplane** is to **pilot** as **bus** is to _____.

4. **Lime** is to **green** as **lemon** is to _____.

5. **Sink** is to **wash** as **oven** is to _____.

Word Box

hard   bake   arm   yellow   driver

Date: _____

Complete each analogy using a word from the Word Box.

1. **Knife** is to **cut** as **pencil** is to _____.

2. **Mouse** is to **squeak** as **dog** is to _____.

3. **Finger** is to **hand** as **toe** is to _____.

4. **Tall** is to **short** as **high** is to _____.

5. **Animal** is to **zoo** as **clown** is to _____.

6. **Wing** is to **bird** as **fin** is to _____.

7. **Juice** is to **drink** as **pizza** is to _____.

8. **Cat** is to **meow** as **lion** is to _____.

9. **Smile** is to **frown** as **up** is to _____.

Word Box

foot	play
hand	circus
elbow	fly
flower	pet
movie	read
fish	arm
write	eat
bark	cook
low	sleep
roar	cut
boy	knee
under	down
laugh	

Roar!

Meow!

analogies

Date: _____

Write the missing word to complete each analogy. Color the words below to help the elephant get to the camel.

1. **Knife** is to **cut** as **broom** is to _____.

2. **Early** is to **late** as **light** is to _____.

3. **Short** is to **tall** as **small** is to _____.

4. **Question** is to **answer** as **empty** is to _____.

5. **Quiet** is to **noisy** as **hot** is to _____.

6. **Shout** is to **whisper** as **wide** is to _____.

7. **Empty** is to **full** as **clean** is to _____.

8. **Boat** is to **water** as **plane** is to _____.

9. **In** is to **out** as **happy** is to _____.

10. **Elephant** is to **trunk** as **camel** is to _____.

sweep · dark · big · drink · hump · full · small · sad · open · cold · knife · sky · heavy · narrow · dirty · warm · out

Vocabulary Practice Test

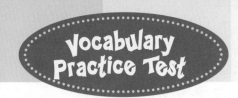

Fill in the bubble next to the correct answer.

1. Which word means the same as **big**?

○ **A** tiny

○ **B** large

○ **C** small

○ **D** lean

2. Which word means the opposite of **cold**?

○ **A** chilly

○ **B** freezing

○ **C** cool

○ **D** hot

3. Which word is a homophone of **write**?

○ **A** weight

○ **B** right

○ **C** wait

○ **D** waste

Vocabulary Practice Test

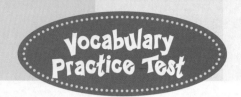

Fill in the bubble next to the correct answer.

4. Which season has the hottest weather?

○ **A** summer

○ **B** winter

○ **C** spring

○ **D** fall

5. Which weather word describes water falling from the sky?

○ **A** snow

○ **B** rain

○ **C** hail

○ **D** blizzard

6. Which word is the name for a bear's baby?

○ **A** kitten

○ **B** cub

○ **C** calf

○ **D** puppy

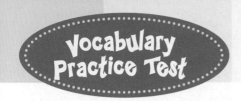

Fill in the bubble next to the correct answer.

7. Which community helper will help you find a good book to read?

- **A** librarian
- **B** police officer
- **C** firefighter
- **D** dentist

8. Which part of a map has a list of symbols and what they stand for?

- **A** compass
- **B** title
- **C** key
- **D** scale

9. Which word is a direction word?

- **A** very
- **B** big
- **C** north
- **D** happy

Fill in the bubble next to the correct answer.

10. Which word describes a shape with three sides?

    ◯ **A**   square

    ◯ **B**   circle

    ◯ **C**   triangle

    ◯ **D**   diamond

11. Which animal lives in the ocean?

    ◯ **A**   octopus

    ◯ **B**   ape

    ◯ **C**   lion

    ◯ **D**   bear

12. Which word completes the analogy?

    Big is to **large** as **tiny** is to _____.

    ◯ **A**   round

    ◯ **B**   huge

    ◯ **C**   full

    ◯ **D**   little

begin	see
start	look
glad	big
happy	large
loud	down
noisy	up
little	under
small	over

diamond	fall
square	summer
octagon	blizzard
triangle	rain
rectangle	snow
circle	sunshine
winter	cloud
spring	sky

bus driver	car
doctor	bike
dentist	truck
firefighter	train
teacher	north
airplane	south
bus	east
ship	west

Answer Key

Alphabet and Handwriting

Page 6-38
Review tracing, copying and writing on each page.

Page 39-40
1. T   2. T   3. g   4. m and q

Vocabulary

Page 42
2. happy   3. noisy   4. small   5. look   6. large

Page 43
2. quiet   3. say   4. story   5. right
6. peek   7. big   8. afraid   9. set
Synonyms are words that have the same meanings.

Page 44
1. up   2. big   3. in
4. wet   5. hot   6. over
7. soft   8. dirty   9. sad

Page 45

Across	Down
1. frown	2. old
4. left	3. north
6. dirty	4. little
9. happy	5. first
11. stop	7. open
12. narrow	8. found
14. smooth	10. across
16. over	13. remember
	15. tall

Page 46
1. doorbell   2. football   3. sunflower   4. cupcake
5. beehive   6. bedtime   7. flowerpot   8. raincoat
9. popcorn   10. toothbrush   11. bookshelf

Page 47

Across	Down
4. bathtub	1. bookshelf
5. fingerprint	2. beehive

7. eyelid   3. underground
8. airplane   4. bedtime
9. toothbrush   6. sunflower
11. sundown   10. doorknob

Page 48
1. hear   2. no   3. two
4. eight   5. scent   6. brake
7. sew   8. mane   9. rode

Page 49
1. dear, deer   2. to, two   3. son, sun
4. cent, scent   5. chilly, chili   6. there, there
7. no, no   8. hare, hair   9. be, bee
10. hear, hear

Page 50
1. star   2. row   3. yard   4. down
5. rest   6. kind   7. train   8. jam

Page 51
1. triangle   2. square   3. diamond   4. circle
5. octagon   6. rectangle   7. circle   8. diamond
9. triangle   10. octagon   11. rectangle   12. square

Page 52
1. square   2. triangle   3. rectangle
4. diamond   5. oval   6. circle

Page 53
1. spring   2. winter   3. autumn
4. summer   5. spring   6. autumn

Page 54
2. hail   3. tornado   4. rain
5. snow   6. sunshine

Page 55

Across	Down
2. bear	1. penguin
5. alligator	3. dolphin
6. ape	4. octopus
7. lion	

Page 56

```
W H A L E E T S Z C T F
L A S E P E Y H B X U I
O F D P R L V A N M R S
B G H O J K L R E K T H
S O C L A M I K U Y L T
T A S D O L P H I N E D
E S E A H O R S E G H F
R R D G J S H R I M P T
```

Page 57

```
g r a s s h o p p e r c
b w e r l a d y b u g r
e y b u t t e r f l y i
e u i k m n a n t b f c
m o t h l j k u y s a k
r t e q a r o a c h o e
b e e t l e y s i m p t
n f h j m o s q u i t o
```

Page 58

1. kitten   2. lamb   3. tadpole   4. duckling
5. fawn   6. cub   7. calf   8. foal
9. chick   10. puppy

Page 59

1. doctor   2. bus driver   3. firefighter
4. dentist   5. teacher   6. librarian;
thank you!

Page 60

```
s h i p a n a
a e t d o b i
i l s v a i r
l i t a k k p
b c a n o e l
o o e r c f a
a p u c a r n
t t r u c k e
r e v h b u s
t r a i n l s
```

Air: airplane, helicopter
Land: van, bus, car, bike, truck, train
Water: sailboat, ship, canoe

Page 61

1. symbol   2. map key
3. north, south, east, west   4. compass rose

Page 62

Across	Down
3. elm	1. west
5. north	2. maple
6. east	4. south
	7. ash

Page 63

1. hard-working   2. honest   3. helpful
4. cooperative   5. kind   6. polite

Page 64

1. hard   2. arm   3. driver
4. yellow   5. bake

Page 65

1. write   2. bark   3. foot
4. low   5. circus   6. fish
7. eat   8. roar   9. down

Page 66

1. sweep   2. dark   3. big
4. full   5. cold   6. narrow
7. dirty   8. sky   9. sad
10. hump

Page 67–70

1. B   2. D   3. B   4. A
5. B   6. B   7. A   8. C
9. C   10. C   11. A   12. D

Congratulations!

SCHOLASTIC Learning Express

I,

_____

am a Scholastic Superstar!

I have completed Handwriting and Vocabulary L1.

Presented on _____

Paste a photo or draw a picture of yourself.